Miracle At Crossroads

Barbara Patterson

No part of this book may be reproduced or transmitted in any form or by any means, electronic or mechanical, including scanning, photocopying, recording, or by any information storage and retrieval system, without permission in writing from the publisher.

Copyright © 2018 by Barbara Patterson. All rights reserved.
Miracle at CrossRoads
published by **Triumph Press**
info@TriumphPress.com

Triumph Press is a resource for those who have the passion to tell their life-stories and change the world. If you have a true and inspiring story to share, visit *www.TrimphPress.com* to learn how we can help you publish and join our library of inspirational books.

Dedication

God, I give you thanks for choosing me to share your goodness, your mercy and your grace. For that I am forever grateful.

To my family, thank you for your love and support. It means a lot to me knowing you believe in my passion to tell this story.

To Pastor Rasheed and Rochelle, thank you for always being there and for allowing me to worship Him in spirit and in truth. As loud as I am, and as loud as I will continue to be, you've always let me do me. Love you forever.

CrossRoads Covenant Church Family, I just want to say THANK YOU!

Barbara Patterson

Foreword
by Reverend Rodney Gadsden

When we hear the word "Miracle" we instinctively, or perhaps immediately, think of the Bible. The Bible is replete with miracles. Imagine a sea opening to form two walls allowing a nation of people to cross over safely on *dry* land to escape enemy pursuit or feeding 5000 men with only five loaves of bread and two fishes (not to mention the leftovers)!! Then there is the account of a virgin immaculately conceiving and giving birth to the Incarnate God. Lastly, the resurrection of the crucified Christ. This specific miracle is still the topic of conversation (and debate) today, more than 2000 years later.

Each of these miracles involved ordinary, everyday people like you and me. Some in impossible situations where answers and solutions were outside their reach. A good question for us is, "Do we believe in miracles today?" When you pray for a miracle, do you believe it can happen for you as it did for Mary and Martha when Jesus raised Lazarus from the dead? The word *Miracle* is defined *as a surprising and welcome event that is not explicable by natural or scientific laws and is therefore considered to be the work of a divine agency.* Another definition is a *highly improbable or extraordinary event, development, or accomplishment that brings very welcome consequences.*

What if we expand our imagination and/or understanding of miracles beyond the Bible? What would it look like for you? In this work, you will see that miracles still happen today. If you've prayed for a miracle but haven't seen it manifest in the manner or timeframe you requested, continue to hold on and trust! As you read this book, I pray your faith will grow, be strengthened or rekindled. In whatever form He chooses, trust the One who still performs miracles. May you be encouraged today!

ONE

One of my favorite songs is, *I Woke up this Morning with my Mind Stayed on Jesus.* March 23, 2018 was like any ordinary day. I got up, had my praise and worship, and ate some oatmeal with walnuts, cranberries, raisins and banana. I was happy because the *Daniel Fast* that I was on with my CrossRoads Covenant Church family was almost over. I could have a cup of coffee and anticipate God doing something great again because the Bible says some things only come out by fasting and prayer! I was excited about the Strength Finders Bible Study that I was able to attend the previous three weeks on Wednesday evenings. It explained a lot of who I am and why I do the things that I do. Strength Finders is a course which guides you to identify your top five strengths, and how to use them most effectively. By learning this, I was able to analyze areas where I would stop, drop and roll for my family!

My first strength is Adaptability. I prefer to go with the flow and don't see the future as a fixed destination. I respond quickly to chaos and circumstances. I make decisions based on facts and move forward with a positive attitude, connected through prayer for God to show me what to do next.

My second strength is Positivity. I have contagious enthusiasm and can get people excited. I encourage them to sign all the way up for Jesus, while my third strength is Belief. I have certain core values that are unchanging. I believe every word of the Bible; holiness is not popular, but it is still right, and I strive to live accordingly.

My fourth strength is Connectedness. I have very strong faith in the links of life; there are no coincidences and every event in life has a purpose. I love to build bridges between people, especially families. My fifth strength is Relator. I find satisfaction in close relationships; these friendships are trusting, caring, close and mutually rewarding.

So, with all that God has gifted me, "What's the problem?" I am terrified to write, but I can speak the story with no problems. I talk to strangers all day. I'm a Realtor with United Real Estate Dallas and an Uber driver. I have shared this miracle with a few people and on every occasion was told that it needs to be a book. On one particular day, I could hear and feel God tell me that it's time to write this book. My response was "Ok" with some apprehension, because I have never written a book or had any interest in writing. I just wanted to tell the story of a Supernatural God who did a Supernatural Miracle using an everyday 43-year-old, single (but engaged) African American mother of two God-fearing young women: Casey and Tia from Dallas, Texas, who love God!

I was driving on my way to Walmart to pick up a client when I began to feel very uneasy in my spirit. I heard the Lord say, "I need you to start writing." I capitulated and replied, "Ok," but I was trying to make an extra $25 dollars because my car note and credit card bills were fast approaching. I'm pretty good at negotiations, so I told the Lord that after I drive four more people, I will call it a day and figure out how to start this process.

As I was in the turn lane, I looked to my right and saw my niece Casey's pink car missing a hub cap. As I watched her go through the light, I heard God say,

"I need you to start writing because you are the only one that can tell the story for me." Now I was scared. I felt like something was about to happen as I picked up the Uber client and helped load many bags of groceries in my car. I started to talk about family, and she told me about her kids and a boyfriend that she had been with for nine years. She confessed that she was terrified to get married. I felt inspired to tell her about God and how this was not the plan that He had for her life. I reminded her how kids mirror what they see, not what you say, as they are little magnets that cling to what's around them. The example you set in front of them will be the road that they will likely follow, and she surly doesn't want them to live in sin.

I continued to feel troubled and before I dropped off that passenger, I accepted another ride request. I helped this client unload my car and gave her an invitation to my church spring revival that was set to start on Sunday, March 25, 2018. I told her, "Good bye," and, "I pray to see you at the revival." Then I headed back out to pick up the request that I just accepted. The drive was about eight minutes away, and I was almost there when my 2016 Chevrolet Malibu did not move. I pressed my foot all the way down on the peddle, but my car was straining, barely moving, so I started praying. I didn't have to rebuke the devil this time, I knew with certainty that this was the hand of God.

I canceled the passenger I was on my way to get and rolled to the right side of the road, praying real loud, *Lord please forgive me! I'm sorry for being disobedient*! As the traffic went by, I prayed for a chance to make a slow turn so I would be out of harm's way. I got to a safe place and turned my car off, deciding in my nervousness what to do next, whether to call roadside assistance, Darius my brother-in-law, or Jesus. I knew that Jesus would help me, even in my ignorance, so I started praying, *God will you please let me get to Chuck Fairbanks Chevrolet*? (That is where I purchased the car, which was about two miles away!)

I started my car and once again His mercy was there. I drove my car on the back streets and got to the dealership in five minutes, at 5:15 pm on a Friday. I explained what was going on and that I also needed an oil change. I relayed that as I put my foot to the gas, very little movement resulted, and I saw a light go off that indicated something about pressure. He told me they couldn't look at it until Monday, and he called for a guy named Ryan to write up a ticket at 5:31. I was in a 2018 Chevy Cruise loaner car for the weekend. It was not a Malibu, but I was so grateful and in awe of God!

I got in the loaner and went straight home, praying and thanking God for being so good to me! I called my friend Nita and told her what happened. She laughed and encouraged me to start writing. I told her how I had no knowledge of how to use a computer nor did I really want to. I was so nervous, I got a tablet and an ink pen instead and started writing. After three pages, I had a few key questions, mainly, "How in the world did anyone write a book before type writers or computers?" My right hand was hurting, my shoulder was stiff, and then I realized I had to get somebody to tell me how to update my unused laptop and find Word or Wordperfect or something like that. I wasn't sure. All I knew was the Lord told me to write a book, and I was going to do it.

I called Casey, my niece, and she agreed to look at my computer. "Auntie, what is your Microsoft password?" was her first question. I laughed a little because I was clueless; I didn't know that I had a password or that I needed one. Casey said, "I need your password for Microsoft!" My response: "What password?" And that was the end of that conversation.

I'm the last person to be writing a book. I am not technology smart, and I'm ok with that. I can take no credit for this story except God called me, and I said, "Yes." I had to get started, so I took some Excedrin, put some Bengay (arthritis cream) on my hands like it was lotion and picked up that pen and tablet again. I wrote another page, then concluded, *God I know that this is not the process that I have to take to write a book. I need a working computer along with some knowledge on how to get started.* I didn't want to be frustrated in the "being about my Father's business." I did what I knew to do; I started praying, *HELP ME, help me please figure this out! I am not dumb!* Then, I starting quoting *The Help* movie, "You is smart; you is kind; you is intelligent!" I laughed at myself and went to bed.

The next morning, my friend Anita called me, "Barbara, I have a computer that you can borrow!" She gave me a few month's dead line, not knowing that she was working for the Lord and unconsciously holding me accountable! I put on my clothes and in 30 minutes was at Anita's house. I told her that I would call Casey and she could get me started, but we still tried together to figure it out. To my surprise, she knew what I did about computers…. Nothing! I came home feeling optimistic but too anxious to wait for

Casey, so I did what I love to do; I opened my Bible to the Book of Joshua and started reading, then praying. I was reminded that everywhere the soles of my feet are placed has been given to me. My confidence was boosted, *Now God, we got this!* Later that evening, my friend LaPortia (who lives in Missouri City) called and I explained my dilemma. She laughed and told me to take a picture of the screen. Then she guided me step by step how to get this book started.

TWO

My name is Barbara Patterson. I have been given this great opportunity to share a story about my sister, Loyce Ann Lewis-Bryant, a beautiful woman of God who chose to love, honor and trust Him. Born July 10, 1967 to Charles and Doris Lewis and raised in Dallas, Texas, we were taught about the Lord at a very young age. My mom would send us by foot to Greater Emmanuel Baptist Church where all seven kids got the basics of trusting God. (Donna, Charles Junior who passed in December 1986, David, Ronald, Barbara with the nick name Net, Loyce and Brian, in birth order)

I really didn't like church because I always got in trouble. I remember a kid sitting behind me that kept pulling my hair. I turned around to tell him to stop, but with a silly grin on his face, I guess he thought

I was playing. Just as soon as I turned around, he would pull again. After a few more pulls, I got up in the middle of service and punched him upside his head until Sister Upchurch came to his rescue and marched me out of church! I was about nine years old. I wasn't taken to the back of the church, but was kicked out to the gravel/dirt parking lot. I was free in my mind to never have to ever come back to church, but reality soon set in.

I couldn't go home without my sisters or brothers, but as heaven would have it, one by one they came to my aide and said, "Girl, you whipped him!" We laughed about how sternly Sister Upchurch grabbed and shook me. I was not phased one bit, but I was mad and carried the side-eye glance for her a long time. So, I learned at a young age to fight for myself.

We continued to grow up in a very strict environment. Mom wouldn't let us run the neighborhood; she made it very clear that after she went to work, we were to have no company. With that said, as soon as she would leave for work, we entertained company. This was the norm. During the summer months, we all would go to Eighth Street Park for free lunch, then after lunch, we would swing, play on the merry go round, have foot races, go swimming and just be kids. In these activities, mom had just one rule: stay together and watch out for each other. With seven of us growing up, hormones all over the place, my mom had a strange but absolute genius way of punishing us; if we got into a fight or an argument about anything, my mom would give us the speech about "we are all that we have" and how she will not allow us to hate each other. So, she would make us hug and kiss on the mouth. It felt like the worst torture. I told her one time that I would rather just take a whipping instead of kissing. Well, I got the requested whipping and still had to kiss. At that time, I was faced with kissing my oldest brother Jr.

We always had our fists balled up for some reason. He was so bossy, mean, and just hateful, always trying to tell me what to do. I was a strong-willed fighter, not one to follow instructions from him. So, in order for me to listen, he would do silly stuff to agitate me. If I felt the least bit threatened, it was "on" and "popping." I would fight him as if I was going to win, and of course I didn't, but I knew what to do to make him mad. I would tell him how ugly he was, and if momma got wind of me talking about him, we would be back to the kissing post.

My sister Loyce and I kissed a lot. I was always meddling because she was a crybaby, and I would make her cry on purpose. She carried her emotions all over the place; if I looked at her funny or said something that she didn't like or commented on an outfit that was a mess, she would scream, "Momma, Net's meddling me!!!" and back to the kissing post we went. But as we continued to grow, the kissing was changed to being sent to the closet or under the bed to stay there until mom came to get us. I really didn't mind the closet or under the bed because I would talk to God and go to sleep. Mom had no idea that these punishments were making me a stronger Christian. Mom would eventually come wake me up because I would always be in bed the next morning.

At the age of 20, Loyce became pregnant with her oldest daughter, Casey Bryant. Six months after Casey was born, she was pregnant with Tia Greer. Being the mom of two young children, she went through postpartum depression. I remember Loyce calling me, crying. She reminded me that I made her a promise to help with the kids. I was just engaged to my second husband, Darryl, so I explained to him that my sister needed me, and for a week or more we had a newborn baby, Tia, while my momma had Casey. This was new to all of us, but with God's help, Loyce came out of depression without taking medicine. I told her to lay the Bible on her head and read it if she could, and she did just that. My sister didn't like taking medicine of any kind; she would hurt first, then if the pain was too bad, she would take medicine, but only as the last option. On the other hand, give me a pill and pillow because I don't like pain.

My sister soon found out that the Word of God was working and as her girls grew, she did what our mom did for us as kids, and would send her girls to church with my mom. In this season, my sister was not in church; she was in the club looking for what the club could never provide. She was seeking a man, and oh my, did she find a bunch of no-car, no-job, no-money, no-nothing type of leaches. She had a heart to help, but didn't have a dime of her own. So, life was tough, trying to make ends meet…. or for the ends to at least look at each other!

During this season, Tia and Casey would go to church with my mom. One day, mom came from church and told us that every Sunday Tia would go to the alter and ask the church to pray for her momma. I was not in a lot of contact with my family; I was in the club too, but I faithfully went to church. I didn't care about what I did on Saturday night, as long as by Sunday morning, I was ready to worship. I would enter the church with the club stamp on the back of my hand from the night before.

We had a different club life. Loyce went to stuff in the hood… holes in the walls where you could BYOB (Bring your own bottle) while I would go to upscale holes in the walls. I really didn't drink a lot and if I did, it was before the club. I would do most of my sipping at home, sometimes smoking weed or a cigarette just for the aroma of being with the click. I would call my sister on occasion to see what was going on and to check on the girls, and from her conversations, she always had "just met a guy." This went on for years. I would always pray for Casey and Tia, asking the Lord to please watch over and protect them from all hurt, harm or danger. This became my everyday prayer; then God would place in my heart to really focus on my family. I would work, go to the club, and pray in that order. After a few more phone calls, I soon realized that things were becoming crazy. My sister was letting the girls stay at home while she partied, or they were at their dad's or grandmothers, if not with a friend or cousins.

I was concerned for their safety, so I had to change my strategy. My prayer-life became first; God told me that it was time to put up my club attire. This was hard for me because I absolutely love to dance. From the time that I walked into the club, I would be on the floor and stay there until the last call for alcohol. Now God had need of me, and I didn't go without a little struggle. I was in the club one night, just getting it, dropping and head bopping. I was dancing with a guy when another man next to me said, "You're not supposed to be in here!" I started laughing and kept on getting it, so on the next song, he wanted to dance with me. I hesitated, but he was cute, so I said "Ok," but I didn't want him to tell me again that I shouldn't be there. He immediately started talking about the Lord, and I got scared. I knew in that moment, I was done. I had my conviction experience, and my club life was over. I went to the rest room and returned to ask him something, but I couldn't find him anywhere. That messed me up; how in the world does a person disappear unless he wasn't supposed to be there either, or was he an angel? I didn't want to know, I said to myself, *Self, we got to get out of here; feet don't fail me now!* I was out the door, walking to my car, not really knowing why in the world the Lord would keep me from dancing, but I had to obey.

I began to fast and pray on a regular basis. I have a heart for my family, friends etc. I asked the Lord *If I have to stop clubbing and focus on Him, will my family be able to worship with me?* He said, "Yes!" I was so excited. I was a member of Pilgrim Rest Baptist Church and loved to worship there. The Lord was dealing with me in a different way; the more I read my Bible, the stronger He got in me. Then one day, the Lord told me that I had to cut away from some close friends; these relationships were very dear to me, but in order to do what God was requiring of me, I had to let them go. In order to walk with Him, because I love my family, if I was going to see a difference, I had to be the difference. I had to get in the presence of God. I believed His word, that the Bible was the only way that I wanted to live, so I became "souled out" for Jesus.

I was still at Pilgrim Rest Baptist Church, and at this time, Loyce was coming to church. I was so excited she joined church and became active in the bereavement ministry and in her Sunday school class. Then, shortly after, my brother David joined, but I didn't see him a lot in church because I went to the 8 am service and he came later. I was just happy that they were with me in worship. Loyce and I attended the early service, and we became very close; but after about a year, I felt God was telling me it was time to leave Pilgrim Rest. I was begging, *No, no, no please God I don't want to go! I love it here! What about my Sunday School class? They'll miss me, and I'll miss them!* But He didn't hear me. I was receiving the same message, "It's time to leave." *Ok Lord, where are we going?*

*Left to right, top to bottom:
Loyce, David, Barbara "Net" and Ronald*

"Net" (Barbara) and Loyce, ages 4 and 6

Loyce and Brian

THREE

On this particular day, my childhood friend, Brenda Gooden, was pregnant and needed some help with house cleaning and laundry. I had been praying for direction as I drove down Pleasant Run Rd in DeSoto, Texas. I heard God say in clear speech, "This is the place that I want you to serve!" I was in front of CrossRoads Covenant Church. I looked to my right and said, *What Lord?* He repeated "This is where I want you to serve." I said, *God, is it a white church?* Because, I really didn't know. But I knew I heard Him, so I continue to Brenda's house and when I got there, I asked her to keep me in prayer because God was calling me from Pilgrim Rest. I told her that I needed direction and she said, "Ok, I'll pray!" and in the same breath she asked me if I have ever heard about CrossRoads Covenant Church. I screamed and told her that was the church that the Lord just told me on my way to her house is where He wants me to serve. She said, "You'll fit right in! The pastor is Josef Rasheed. He is married and has some young kids." This was my confirmation. On the following Sunday, I went to CrossRoads Covenant Church, not knowing what to expect. I got a great welcome; worship was good, and most importantly, the word preached was good.

On this particular Sunday, Pastor Rasheed had on military gear: a green t-shirt with a hat to match. He preached about being in the military and how once you're enlisted in service, you don't get the opportunity to tell the commander in charge where you want to go or serve; you only go where you are stationed. I joined church on the following Sunday. They were having a fellowship meal, and I was invited to the front of the line because I was a first-time visitor. I ate my food, talked to a few people and felt at home. God called me here to serve, and I was in for an adventure that would change the life of my entire family.

I got involved immediately. I started going to church, Sunday School, Wednesday night Bible study and noon-day prayer and Bible study. I loved this small group of believers, and the theme was *Where God's*

Love Connects with your Life. I believed with all of my being that God's love was there. Before God placed me at CrossRoads, I had a few specific requirements in mind regarding what I needed in a church family. I asked God to put me somewhere that served communion every week; I needed my Pastor to know my name and a church that believed in fasting and prayer. When I found my prayers were answered, I knew that God had intricately placed me at this House of Worship. I was ready to see the unexpected from God.

After joining CrossRoads, I became a Volunteer Chaplin for Charlton Methodist Hospital. I felt like in the hospital I was sure to win souls for the Kingdom of God, and I was building my prayer-life there. I would go to the volunteer center, and they would normally have a list of patients who had high blood pressure or some other minor illnesses. I anticipated going in the rooms of the patients to just give them some hope and tell them about the goodness of the Lord.

Loyce lived about five minutes from the hospital on Cherry Street in Duncanville, Texas, so on days that I volunteered, I would go to her home to hang out, or if I was going to Bible Study, I would go to her home early enough to just talk. One day in August

2009, I had just come over with a hamburger, fries, and a shake from Braum's (my favorite burger joint), and we were sitting at the table talking about Jesus because it's was what we loved to do. God was always making a way. There was a knock on the door in the middle of the day, so Loyce answered it. There stood a Caucasian woman named Kim from a local funeral home, dripping with sweat, who was going door to door selling insurance policies for burial needs with an almost joyful expectancy. Loyce invited her in and offered her some water. Kim said that she had been knocking for a while and that Loyce was the only person that let her in and offered water. Kim explained the reason for her visit, which was to sell funeral policies and Loyce said, "Oh yes ma'am, I'm interested!" She looked at me and said, "Net, I need this because I'm not going to be here." I said, "Where you going?!" and she said, "I won't be here." I said, "Really?!" and then I gave my response to the sales woman, "Well, I don't need it because I'm going to be here for a long time!"

Kim started explaining the policy, and I continued to eat my burger; then they started talking about being cremated. Loyce said, "When I get cremated, y'all can get jewelry to wear me around your necks!" I said, "I wish!" Kim started laughing and explained that they had necklaces and bracelets for family members to put the ashes in to always be connected to your loved ones. While they were completing the paper work, Casey came home and I told her what her mom had done, but Casey was not interested and kept walking. After they finished the paperwork, Kim left. Loyce was so happy, she said, "Now my kids can put me away and have a few dollars left over." As I look back, I recall she often said, "When I'm on life support, that's going to be it. Don't try to keep me here." She said this at her class reunion. It never made sense, but apparently she had a conversation with God and that's just how it happened.

Loyce was still at Pilgrim Rest serving, and I was so ashamed to tell her that I was leaving. The first Sunday I missed church, she was shocked because I never miss church, no matter what, unless I'm out of town, which was rare. I called her and said, "Girl, the Lord has called me from Pilgrim Rest." I told her about CrossRoads and how I wound up there. She said, "Net, I'm not following you to another church!" I said, "Ok, I understand," but I really didn't. I enjoyed worshipping with my sister; we were true worshippers. We sang loud and helped the preacher preach. I would invite Loyce for different events, and for a while, she just ignored me, but God allowed a situation to take place that would get her there.

One of our church members, Michael Rocquemore, lost his wife to cancer. Her name was Jackie, and we were good friends. After Jackie passed, we all knew that Michael needed somebody to keep him company. I told Mike about my sister, Loyce, that she was trying to really walk and live for God, and he was interested. They met and immediately started dating. Loyce and Mike were a good match. She taught him how to dress. (He was not really into fashion but she was.) They would go to the thrift store. (She called it the "hookup." Loyce would say, "Look at this! I hooked him up, and it was all good!") After Loyce started dating Mike, she started visiting CrossRoads and fell in love with God and His people at this church. She joined CrossRoads shortly after.

We had the annual Woman's Tea, and I didn't tell anyone that Loyce decorated for a living. She worked 15 years for Jeff & Yvette Patton (Patton's Christmas Trees and Decorations by Yvette). My sister learned how to make anything pretty. She brought in all types of fancy items to put on her table, and it was beautiful. I remember two of our members took down their items because Loyce's decorations were so superior.

Loyce told them that she would help their tables after she put the finishing touch on hers. All I could do was laugh because they were mad. Loyce helped anybody that needed her assistance because decorating is what she did. She was a *TALENTED* decorator. She was also the hands that decorated for Mrs. Ann James, a generous and dear friend of our family, who said that Loyce was the only person that made her throw things away. She considered Loyce to be her best friend. I think she won first place, and I loved it.

CrossRoads is a small, family-oriented church; we love and embrace people no matter what, and Loyce felt that love as well. One Sunday, Pastor Rasheed called Loyce by name from the pulpit and that was "it" for her. She said, "Net, your pastor knows my name!" I said, "Girl, he knows everyone by name. God anointed him with a gift of remembering names, places, and situations."

Then came the chili cook off season, and Loyce & Michael decided to give it a go. I wasn't there, but I heard that the chili was real good and they won first place. I was all grins again. They even received a trophy. Loyce continued to serve, and I saw the gradual change in her life. I was at her home one day, sitting together at the table, and she told me how good

God had been to her. Loyce said, "Net, guess what? I quit smoking weed!" We had a praise party. Then she told me that Mike was the only man she ever dated that she didn't cheat on, and I was dumbfounded. I said, "What?!" She said, "Yep, in every relationship that I have ever been in, I have cheated." I was choked up because God was working in her life, and I could see it.

My sister was a sharp dresser. She had really good stuff that normally came from a high-end resale shop. On occasion, I would ask her for something, and she would have to think about it. One day, she came to church in a red pant suit that was so pretty. I said, "Oh my God, I love that suit!" She said, "You can have it!" And I was all teeth! I said, "What!? Don't play with me!" She said, "I'm not playing, after I have it cleaned, you can have it!!" I was so excited that I went to her house right after church and said, "You might change your mind, so I need my suit now." (hahaha) Then she went to her closet and pulled out a large purse case and said, "You can have any of these purses. I'm not going to need them." I was confused. Loyce was letting me have my pick of any purse that I wanted. Going forward, she would also give me something any time that I came to the house. She gave me a coffee cup, a pair of shoes, and a sister marque just to name a few items. Loyce was so generous with all of her stuff, I should have known that God was up to something, but my spiritual maturity was in growth process, and I can truly say that I missed it.

Loyce and Michael had been dating for about nine months, and they made the decision to get married. She was so excited; they had a date set for November 2010. We were trying to figure out if they were going to have a church wedding or hold it in the backyard. I said, "You should have a church wedding!" but she wanted to party and figured out that she couldn't party at church. I said, "Have a church wedding, then bring the party to the backyard." Michael's lease was coming to an end, and he was planning on moving in before marriage. I was so disappointed. I said, "Don't do it! Please allow your girls to see something different." But both of them were struggling financially, so they figured that they could save some money if they shacked. I started praying on a regular basis concerning this matter. She eventually told me to mind my business and, being the older sister, I felt like this was my business. So, I did what I do best. I prayed.

Loyce

Loyce and Michael Roquemore

FOUR

July 2010, Loyce told me that she had a headache. I asked her if she had high blood pressure and she said that she did, but that she didn't want to take the medication. She worried that the medicine would affect her kidneys in the long run. I told her that I didn't know how true that was, but she needed to take it anyway.

Thursday, July 8, 2010, I woke up not feeling my best self. I got out of the bed and noticed that the right side of my body was tingling. It was that feeling you get when your foot falls asleep. I immediately went to get my mom's blood pressure machine and checked my blood pressure. It was 201/115, and I knew that I needed to get myself to the emergency room. I told my mom what it said, but I wanted another opinion. My brother was dating a girl named Princess, and I asked her to ride with me to the fire station to get my blood pressure checked again there. It took us about two minutes to arrive. I told them how I was feeling, and they hooked me up to their machine. The paramedic looked at me as if to say, "Why did you come here first?" The home blood pressure was better than the fire station's; it was much higher there, and I was dizzy.

They wanted to take me to the ER by ambulance, but I had Princess with me. They told me to let her drive my car, but there was no way in the world I was doing that. Princess was a drug addict with no driver's license. I just took her because my sweet momma said I shouldn't go by myself. The paramedics told me to go straight to the hospital. I went back home first, dropped Princess off, and drove to Methodist Hospital on Colorado Blvd. I parked my car, walked in a blur to the counter, and gave them a piece of paper that was given to me from the fire station with my blood pressure reading. Within one minute, I was in a wheelchair. They rolled me to the back and took my blood pressure again. It was higher than at the fire station. Then I started asking, "Lord, is this it? Are you ready for me, God? I ain't ready for you!" and I prayed as best I could.

I looked up and there were about five white coats trying to figure out what's going on with me. I really didn't know. They asked how long I've had high blood pressure. I told them, "I'm just finding out today." The more they talked, the higher my pressure went up. They immediately gave me an IV in my arm to start medication to bring it down. After about three hours, it finally started dropping. I was feeling normal and ready to go home, but because they had a very hard time getting it down, they recommended that I stay the night for observation. I was like *WHAT!?* I really didn't want to spend the night in the hospital. I called my mom and told her that I was staying the night and to please not come because I was exhausted and just wanted to sleep. This was a Thursday, and she insisted on coming. Mom said she was passing by the hospital after work. I said, "I know momma, but I don't want any visitors!"

I called the church to ask them to pray. I called Loyce and said, "Girl, I'm in the hospital with high blood pressure!" I told her that this was the first time I ever felt like this, but I was getting better. Then I remembered begging her to please, please take her medicine. I told her that if she felt like it's not the correct brand or dosage, she could get her doctor to change the prescription. She said, "Net, I'm drinking vinegar for my blood pressure." I said, "Girl, that's the saltiest thing in the world!!!" But she stuck to her belief. I told her that I heard everything she said, but I was going to get my prescription filled because I wanted to be here for a long time.

The day after I was released from the hospital, I got a phone call from my ex-boyfriend Paul. He wanted to know Loyce's address because they had a history of celebrating their birthdays together. Paul's day is July 6; Loyce's is the 10th. I gave him the address and called Loyce to see if she was home for him. I told her that he was on Cherry street. Once again, she wasn't feeling good, and I told her that I wanted to come over there because I wanted to celebrate with them, but I really wanted to come and check her blood pressure myself. However, I wasn't feeling on top of my game, but I would have gone if she gave me the ok. I talked to her until Paul got in the house. This was the one thing that was consistent in her life: her brother-in-law is who he had always been to her, good company and conversation, and she was so happy.

July 10, 2010 was Loyce's 43rd birthday. Life was so good! She was engaged to be married to Michael Roquemore and her daughter, Casey, had just moved back in. She had a point to prove that she could survive on her own. Although she was only five minutes away, the point was proved. Tia had graduated from beauty college and money was tight, but that wasn't new. I got a phone call from Pastor and Rochelle Rasheed that they wanted to visit me after my high blood pressure scare. I gave them directions to the house and hung up my phone. I told my brother, Ronald, that I needed him to be on his best behavior, that my pastor and wife was coming and he was shocked. He said, "I didn't know that the church still visits people!" I said, "This is why I attend CrossRoads. My pastor and his wife know me. I don't have to make an appointment to see him or her." I also assured Ronald that I had their phone numbers.

The visit was short and to the point. They came to pray with me and this made my day. I love my church family. CrossRoads is a faith-based, miracle-believing, Holy Ghost (Spirit) filled church, and I was ready to see a miracle. I asked God to show me a miracle. (Be careful about asking for miracles, it will normally cost you something!) I was so excited because Prayer 24 was coming soon. This is the time when the church would open for 24 hours with a member assigned to lead each prayer hour. We had a format to use, but you could also do what the Holy Spirit instructed.

August 2010, I was believing God was about heal somebody… anybody. "God, just do it!" During this season, I was the facilitator for noon-day prayer and Bible study. Three of our faithful church members needed a touch from God and the church was in prayer for their healing. The week of Prayer 24, I was in prayer, and I heard God say that he would heal. I really didn't know what that entailed, but I was ready. It was about to go down. I was singing songs of worship, *Our God is Awesome*, and I was looking for a miracle, too excited for my own good.

Friday night is when the prayer would start, going from 6pm to 6pm Saturday. My sign-up time was always early morning, between 1am-4am. This is the time when the earth is silent, and I can hear Him better, with no distractions. I always fast before Prayer 24 because I need to be empty for me to receive a filling from Him. I started out hungry and really didn't feel like praying, but this is what I came to do, so I asked God to help me get through this hour. After a song and scripture reading, I remember kicking off my sandals and walking around the sanctuary, praying in tongues, and I knew without a doubt that God healed someone from the noon-day Bible study group.

I was asking God to heal each of them in an all-in-one healing because they all needed a touch from God, and all three of them had a heart condition, congestive heart failure or something to do with the heart. Sunday morning after Prayer 24, my friend for over 20 years, Tammy Waters, came to visit CrossRoads for the first time. When Loyce came in, Tammy said, "Oh my goodness, Loyce, you are glowing! You must be in love!" Then, without hesitation, Loyce said, "Tammy, I've been with God." Loyce had a short cute hair cut with her make up flawless and a glitter-green eye shadow, a green multicolor blouse, and a lime green skirt. She was so beautiful. I could also see the presence of God on her. Praise and worship is our high point of the day, and on this particular Sunday, our praise and worship team sang William McDowell's *I Give Myself Away so You can use Me*. I experienced the very presence of God.

Janet Gadsden, our praise and worship leader, is anointed to bless us in worship all the time, and I love God for blessing us through her. Tom Rogers was literally crying tears because he needed a miracle. His heart was in congestive heart failure and in the middle of worship, Loyce looked at me and said, "Net, God is going to bless Tom with a heart!" and I agreed, "Yes He is!" After church, I went to Tom and talked a few minutes sharing with him what Loyce told me. I said, "Tom, God is going to bless you with a new heart." With tears in his eyes from crying, he said he believed that God would bless him.

I enjoyed the time after church. Loyce cooked, and I was hungry! She was telling me the Sunday menu when Rod and Debra Henderson were trying to figure out their plans for a meal. Rod teasingly asked Loyce if she could really cook, and her reply was inviting them to come find out. She cooked all day Saturday in preparation for Sunday. Loyce cooked fried chicken and red beans, then after we got to the house, Casey made corn bread in a loaf pan. It was all good. I love hot sauce on most of my food, and my sister was so bossy that she got mad at me for needing hot sauce on my beans and chicken as well. She said I was messing up the taste, but I assured her that my taste was used to the heat! After eating, I normally go home, but on this particular day, I decided to sit and talk with Debra, Rod, and Michael. Loyce left to go to her class reunion meeting (Franklin D. Roosevelt 1985).

When she got back, I had made myself comfortable on the couch. Loyce said her head was hurting so we got the blood pressure machine to see if her blood pressure was high. It wasn't, so I continued to relax.

We got on the couch together and talked for a long time. Ronald called earlier to ask me to come pick him up from Methodist Hospital because on the Thursday previous, his girlfriend, Princess, had a stroke and was paralyzed on her right side. I told him that I wasn't ready to leave Loyce's house, but I would come after I finished my visit. I sat a little longer having girl talk until a few hours later when Ronald called again. As before, I really wasn't ready to leave, but I'd be on my way. While I was driving, I said to myself, "You have never stayed at Loyce's house that long after church!" I felt a sense of something that I will never be able to explain, perhaps it is what some describe as "impending doom."

I arrived at Methodist Hospital to find Ronald sitting at the bus stop. I asked him about Princess's condition, and he said she would need to go to rehabilitation after she got out. I told him that I wasn't ready to leave my sister's, but since he kept calling, there I was!

Loyce was always so bright and cheerful

Pastor Josef and Rochelle Rasheed

FIVE

On Thursday, August 12, 2010, I was getting breakfast ready for my nieces when the cell phone rang. I looked to see the name "Loyce Bryant" appear on the screen and said to the girls "Yeah, its Aunt Loyce!" When I answered the phone, all I heard on the other end of the line was a horrible scream and crying from my niece, Tia, saying, "Aunt Net, my momma just passed out! Can you please come?" She told me they were at Charlton Methodist, and I exclaimed, "I'm on my way!" I yelled to my mom who was in the kitchen trying to get ready for work. I was in a calm panic. I hastily told her, "Tia called and Loyce has passed out." I immediately called Monica, the mother of the nieces I was watching and said, "You have to come back to get the girls, Tia called and said that Loyce passed out!"

I was out the door. I had a 1995 Honda Accord that needed a new transmission and the air was not blowing at its full capacity. It also had over 200 thousand miles and counting. The car was smoking bad while I was driving and dialing phone numbers. I called the church first. Terri Shaw answered in her always soothing, happy tone. I explained, "Terri, I just got a call that Loyce has passed out. I need you to call anybody that knows how to pray!" Then I called Debra and Rod Henderson, told them what happened, and to start praying. I called my cousins, Bishop Kenneth and Ann Mack, and expressed the urgency, "We needed God to move!"

I was in the parking lot of the hospital when Rodney Gadsden called me. I told him that I really didn't know what happened, but I would call him back when I found out. I went into the hospital, sweating in my short-shorts, a yellow shirt, and red sandals, looking like I just got off the stripper pole. I reached the desk and told them who I was there to see. As they were buzzing me in, the Chaplain was there beside me. I didn't know him, although this is the hospital where I volunteer. He was a young African American male around 40 years old, very quiet with great compassion. We walked to the back and, as I turned the corner, Tia was hysterical. My nephew,

Reverend Donald Ray Parish Jr. (Monica's Husband), was already there praying. He said they were getting ready to Care Flight her to Methodist Dallas. She was non-responsive.

About 10 minutes later, Monica came in and asked if I could go to the car to watch the girls because my mom needed to come in. I went outside, and it was hot as crap. I told mom that they were getting ready to Care Flight Loyce to Methodist. I continued to make and receive calls. I called my brother, David, who was working in Cleveland, Ohio, and then Brian, who was also at work. Monica called her sister, Katrina, who worked for CPS, and Ronald was already at the hospital as his girlfriend, Princess, was in the hospital because of the stroke that happened the previous Thursday. Monica made arrangements for Brenda Gooden to get the girls, and they were hungry. Don came to the car and got the girls to take to Brenda. I went back inside the hospital to see how long it would take for the helicopter to get there. I walked and prayed, looking like I knew nothing about Jesus, then I started speaking in tongues, "Lord Jesus, we need you to help Loyce open her eyes. Help us Lord, in the name of Jesus, have mercy on us Lord! We need a miracle!" I prayed on and on until I saw the helicopter land.

They came in and did the evaluation. I asked if one of us (me or my mom) could ride in the helicopter with her. They said we couldn't; there was only room for the doctor and hospital staff. I remember my hand trembling and heart racing, signing for the helicopter paramedics to take her to the Methodist hospital. I had confidence that she would pull through. I had faith in my God, that He was in control. We watched them load Loyce up and roll her to the tarmac with care and attention. Then they were finally in the air. I watched until I could no longer see the helicopter, praying and speaking in tongues. Finally, I looked down at myself and said, "Lord, you let me come to this hospital looking like a hooker! I got to go home and change clothes… CrossRoads is not ready for all this!"

I called Terri back (the church secretary) and told her that Loyce was flown to Methodist, and I had hope. I would not let my mouth say that it didn't look good. On my way home, I began to have a real talk with God. I wanted to know *What's going on?!* I got no answer, but felt a peace that surpassed my small understanding. I got home, hot as a ghost pepper, and took a quick shower, then continued to remind God of His promise: *I will never leave you nor forsake you.* I continued to pray and took a few minutes to just "be."

I was ready to go to the hospital in about 20 minutes. The drive was short as I lived about five minutes from the hospital. I parked without paying attention. I was trying to get in there as soon as possible. I got to the neurology department where some of the members from CrossRoads were already there: Kyle Royster and Richard Dean. Then others showed up: Rochelle Rasheed, Rodney Gadsden, Debra and Roderick Henderson, Cheryl Smith, Jodi Cuppy, Charles Greer, Paris Doss, Terry McIntyre, Clio Clark, Alvenia (BB) Clewis, Terri Shaw, Viola and Kenneth Fox. My momma asked me, "Who are all these people?" I told her that they are from my church. The waiting area was full.

My mom's sisters showed up: Aunt Josephine, Aunt Betty and Aunt Evelyn. All were just in shock. The doctor came out to give us an update and explain that they were in the process of running a brain scan to see if there was any activity. We waited for the door to open, holding our breath, just to see them take her to another area in the hospital for this test. After about 30 minutes, the team of doctors came back past us with Loyce. We couldn't really see her because of all the equipment. My niece, Katrina, came with one of her co-workers. I was also trying to call Casey as she was in training for her first teacher's job and was scared to leave because it was her first real job. I said, "Girl, yo momma is on life support! I don't care about that job; you need to get her as soon as you can!" I called David back to give him an update. He was in the process of getting a flight from Cleveland, Ohio back to Dallas. My sister Donna came in with her husband, Darius, in shock. Then Brian, the youngest, came with his wife, Tomica, who was a true friend to Loyce. She was in tears. The word got out on social media that Loyce was in ICU at Methodist, and if anyone wanted to see her, they should come. Jackie Loud, her best friend since elementary, was there. She was at the bed tapping Loyce on the face, crying, asking her to please open her eyes. Francine Walker, Keith and Brenda Jennings, Joe and Jane Lyon, along with my mom's pastor Burley Hudson were also there. Kevin Bryant (Loyce's ex-husband and Casey's dad) with his wife Toni, Robert Greer (Tia's dad), and Michael Rocquemore, her fiancé, were all crying.

People were there that my mom and Loyce worked for including Yvette Patton and Ann James. Yvette told me that in December, after a hard job of decorating the Christmas of 2009, Loyce told Yvette that this was her last year of decorating. I don't know if it was a voice of frustration or one of *"It's a wrap,"* like she knew she wouldn't be there the next year. I called my best friend, Kim Terrell-Fisher, at her job. I tried her cell phone and no answer, then I called the dealership as she was working for Mercedes Benz. I called and exclaimed, "I have an emergency phone call for Kim Terrell!" I could hear Kim in the back ground say, "I don't like emergencies!" Prior to calling Kim, I called Tammy Waters, so Tammy was already enroute to get Kim. When Kim got on the phone, I told her what was going on and she said, "I'm on the way!"

I was in the hall pacing when Tammy and Kim came in. Tammy said, "Net, I just saw Loyce on Sunday. She was glowing. It didn't look like anything was wrong." I shrugged my shoulders and we hugged. We walked to the room to see Loyce. Kim commented that she looked like she's asleep. There was peace on her face. We continued to have small talk, trying to figure out what was happening. A nurse came in and said we didn't have to leave. She was just doing some routine charting. I went to the window and in the corner on the ledge was a pigeon, bird, or a dove, (not sure which, but it was just there). I tapped on the window and said, "Are you ok?" I remember praying for the bird. After the nurse left, I was asked if we could come out so other people could come in, because the hospital staff said that only two people were permitted to be in there at a time. There were five of us in the room. I went back to the crowded waiting area and around the corner, I could hear Tia screaming for her daddy. "I want my daddy! I need my daddy!" and thank God he was there. I looked at Sis. Rasheed and said, "Somebody needs to take her home!" She said, "No, just let her cry; she's hurting."

Casey, Loyce and Tia

SIX

We were getting ready to have our first meeting with the neurologist when he came in with no emotions, just a smug, uncompassionate attitude. He said with disgust, "How long has she had high blood pressure?" We all had the same answer.... we didn't know. The doctor informed us Loyce had suffered a brain hemorrhage and that there was no brain activity. As soon as the doctor said that, I heard God say, "I'm going to do a miracle!" and I got so excited. I said with certainty, "I just heard God say that He was going to do a miracle." The doctor was looking at me like I was crazy, as was my entire family. I left the room with a knowing that God was up to something BIG. I kept walking and saying with a loud voice, "God is going to do a miracle!" It felt like I heard crickets chirping with the shocked looks that I was receiving. I looked at Debra Henderson and said, "It ain't over!" and she said, "Ok, I'll believe with you!!" She was the only one that did.

I got frustrated with all the crying and screaming so I decided to go to another floor in the hospital to pray. I said, "God, did they just not hear me say that you are going to do a miracle?" I prayed until I was hot. I have never, ever in all of my life prayed and pleaded with God to totally heal and restore as I did that day. I went back up to be with my family and after about 30 minutes, someone asked me where I had been, and I said, "Praying."

I started praying for other people and families that were in ICU. There was a young man that had a brain injury from a motor cycle accident. I went in the room as if I knew them and asked if I could pray with them. Amidst tears and a lot of pain, they agreed. I remember the mom saying, "I never liked him having a motorcycle." She always feared that he would lose his life doing what he loved. I continued to walk and pray. I saw Pastor Leonard Davis from Galilee Baptist Church as he was there because one of his church members was in ICU from a brain injury; so, I went in her room and prayed with him. Then he came to my sister's room and prayed for her. I was asking God, *Why are your children not taking care of themselves? I don't understand.* I muttered to myself, *If you are diagnosed with any disease, what is in your mind to tell you that medicine is not needed?*

I started praying for women to take better care of themselves. I said, *God, this is not fair! You let a crack head (Princess) live who just had a stroke and was full of drugs. They found so much crack and liquor in her system that she shouldn't be here; and You allowed her to walk in here, paralyzed on one side, but You let her live!!* I was talking all kind of smack to God, and I'm so glad that He can handle it. God told me that Princess wasn't ready to go anywhere.

It was late, and I was exhausted, but hopeful. It was time to go home and try to process. I was in the parking lot and literally had a hard time walking. I felt like I was drunk and drained all at the same time, plus I was still crying. The hospital security patrol car was going by and could tell that I needed help, so he pulled up next to me and asked if I was ok. I said, "Sir, my sister is on life support, and I don't know where I parked my car!" He said it happens all the time and told me to get in. Then he started driving, and I looked over at his name badge. The last name was Quilens. I asked him if he knew Rhonda Quilens. He said with a slight laugh, "Yes I do, she's my ex-wife."

and I said, "Oh my goodness, Rhonda and I attend the same church!" He took me to my car after a few circles in the parking lot. I thought, *God, you allowed Rhonda's ex-husband to be the person that would help me in my weariest hour!*

The next day, August 13, 2010, I had an appointment with Parkland Hospital at 8 am in the morning. With a heavy heart and a lot of tears, I wanted to cancel the appointment, but it took me so long to get on the schedule, I didn't want to miss it. I drove to the hospital in shock. I got to the sign-in desk and sat down to wait for my name to be called. When my name came up after a few minutes, I sat down and the regular questions were asked: name, date of birth and if all of my information was correct. The lady asked me if Loyce Bryant was still my emergency contact, and I burst out in a full flow of tears. I snotted and fell apart. I told her, "No ma'am, my sister is on life support, and I will need to change that information. I'll be going back to the hospital after I leave this appointment." She came from behind the desk and just hugged me.

I was scheduled for a sonogram to see if there was a tumor big enough to need a hysterectomy or if I should just live with my chronic pain. The sonogram took place and the young man that did the sonogram said that the tumor was eight centimeters. I said, "Ok," but was in no shape to discuss anything more. I knew we had a funeral to prepare for, and I had my nieces to support. I prayed for God to help me get through my dilemma and not have this pain while I was enduring the pressure of losing my sister. After the sonogram, the doctor assured me that I would eventually need a hysterectomy, but I disagreed. I felt a peace that I can't explain, and I told the doctor that God was going to heal me. I would be a testimony of His healing. She looked at me like I was crazy… I looked at her the same way, like she was crazy. I said, "Doctor, I understand the facts, but I know God is in control and I don't feel like a surgery is what I'm supposed to do."

Top left to right: Brian, Loyce, Net, Ronald, David, Donna
Bottom: Charles and Doris

SEVEN

I left Parkland Hospital and drove straight to Methodist Hospital. I felt like a nonpaid employee. It was about 10 am when I arrived. I was exhausted because I got no sleep the night before. I walked into the waiting area to see everyone except Casey, as she decided to go to her workshop. I was so confused. We were also waiting for David to get in from Cleveland. I called Casey and told her that the doctors were going to talk to us, and that she needed to come because she is the oldest, and it is her responsibility to be there. She arrived in about 30 minutes.

I was still praying, just asking God to give us something. Soon it was time to meet the doctor because everybody had arrived. Sister Rasheed was there to represent Pastor Rasheed because he was out of town for camp with the kids from church. A lot of the members were there from the day before with a few extra people. The doctor entered with no emotions at all, no sympathy, just a matter-of-fact attitude. I was lost in my feelings and not interested in his update. I could hear God telling me that He was going to work a miracle, and I started sharing what I heard. I looked directly at the doctor and said, "God is going to do a miracle!" The doctor said that Loyce was brain dead; there was no brain activity at all.

I pronounced again to the tight, full-to-capacity waiting room that God said He was going to do a miracle. I started walking and telling anybody that would listen, "God is going to do a miracle!" Everybody was in a stupor, as if they were hard of hearing. I thought to myself in that moment, "If I am ever in any trouble, God please let me get somebody that knows You and make sure they can hear You, and make sure they can pray, no matter what!" I was looking at people that go to church standing before me, clearly showing they had absolutely no belief. I was amazed, "Where is your faith?" I demanded. They were crying and I was mad because I was the only one that believed God. I looked at Richard Dean and said, "God is going to do a miracle!" I was so sure of it that it made good sense to me. He quietly followed and watched. Many people were in the hall, when all of a sudden, I heard God again. He called me by name, "Barbara…" *Yes, Lord?* He then asked me a question that made me almost lose my mind. "If I don't do what you're asking me to do, will you still trust me?"

I told Richard, who was still beside me, that God said He wants me to still trust Him even if he doesn't do what I want. I started screaming and crying. I implored God, *What in the world could you do? I want her to get up!* I was pleading with God. I had no doubt that He could do it, but He just asked me to trust Him with the same question, "Will you still trust me?" I started cussing to myself. I said some 4, 5, and 6 letter words that have absolutely nothing to do with God or the Bible. I said, *God, this is not fair! You just let a nasty, filthy crack-head that had too many drugs in her system live to walk up here, someone who didn't go to church nor did she care anything about You.* I asked the Lord to please just give me a minute. I was saying, *Wait, wait, wait!* I was a mess with everybody else.

I felt like God had let me down. I was in a pain that I thought would kill me; it hurt so bad. I had a hard time breathing. While I was in my feelings, Southwest

Transplant Alliance had been notified. This is the organization that handles organ transplants. They match patients that best fit the deceased patient's organs. It is based on the registry of patients that are waiting for an organ. I was not in on this process because I went to another floor to pray again. I was told that Southwest Transplant asked Casey if she knew of anybody that was in need of organs. Casey's cousin's wife needed a kidney, my mom's best friend Margie needed a kidney, and Reverend Rodney Gadsden, who was there, told them that one of our members, Tom Rogers, needed a heart. Reverend Gadsden called Tom to get his hospital information because Tom was not on a transplant list as he was 71 years old, which is over the age limit for a transplant recipient. Also, Tom was not strong enough the week before, according to his doctors, but God had other plans.

When I came back up from praying, with a quiet whisper, Reverend Gadsden looked at me and said, "They are getting ready to see if Tom is a match for Loyce's heart." In that very instant, I knew that this was the miracle I had been praying for; but if I had known that my sister, friend, worship partner, secret teller, and cook would be the sacrifice, I would not be writing this story at all.

Southwest Transplant contacted Saint Paul Hospital and gathered the information needed to see if he was a match. In the meantime, I called Tom on the phone. He was crying because I was crying. He asked about Loyce's blood type and I said, "Whatever your blood type is, that's what her's is." We talked a few more minutes before I hung up my phone and began to worship God. This was all I had left. I went back in the room where Loyce was and said, "Well, this is it. I believe Tom is about to get his miracle. They still had some testing to do. My niece, Monica, my brother, David, and his friend, Kevin, were in the room as I went back to the window to see the bird from before still sitting in that same position. I wondered if it was hurt and while I was watching, the bird lifted up her wings for a good stretch and up under her wings were some babies. When I saw this, the Holy Spirit hit me like a huge bolt of lightning. I began to straight worship. I cried, spoke in tongues, and was amazed at what I experienced. New life was about to start for all of us because of Loyce's passing. I didn't know what that entailed, but I was ready.

A female Chaplain came in and asked if we needed prayer. Then she began to talk about the presence of God; she observed the peace in the room, and told us that there is a huge difference when a believer passes verses a non-believer. We chatted for a few minutes, then she left. I walked away from the hospital, headed home to pack a bag to spend the night with Casey and Tia. I got in my sister's bed and was wide awake, exhausted, and a little mad, still thinking, "If only she had taken the blood pressure medicine, she would still be here!" I finally dozed off only to wake up a short time later to literally see her in the hall way of her bedroom. Loyce wore a long white flowing night gown and was smiling, and now I was both scared and mad. *What in the world is she smiling at? I'm about to lose my mind and she's smiling!* Then it came back to my mind that we had a conversation recently about her not being here. She was smiling because she was with Jesus.

I had a hard time going back to sleep. I tossed and turned the rest of the night. Then the house phone rang. It was one of the church members from Pilgrim Rest calling to speak with her because she could not believe the information that was on Facebook. I told Frances Trotty, "Yes ma'am, Facebook is telling the truth this time!" We talked for a few minutes, then I said, "The phone is ringing. I'll talk with you later!" I was in the explaining-what-happened-mode most of the morning. As I was standing in the kitchen, Loyce's cell phone rang and the name "Darren Powell" appeared. He was a friend of Loyce's for many years. I answered the phone and we said our "hello's" and "how are you's." Darren said he was working as a truck driver and something just told him to call and check on Loyce. I told him to pull over, "I need you to get off the road for a minute." He said, "No, I'm good. What's up?"

I said, "Darren, Loyce is gone." Confused, he asked, "Whatchu mean by gone?!" I told him she passed on yesterday, and he just started screaming "No, no, no, man, no!!!" Then he was trying to pull over, and I started crying again because he was crying. We talked for a few minutes until I made sure he was ok to continue driving. After about 20 minutes or so, I told him that the phone was ringing, and I had to go, but I would keep him posted on the funeral arrangements.

Saturday afternoon, I was on my way home from Loyce's house when my cell phone rang. I was at Highway 67 and Kiest Blvd, approaching I-35 when my phone went off. It was Rochelle Rasheed asking where I was. I said, "On my way home." Then she told me that Tom was on his way to the hospital to get Loyce's heart. I started crying and laughing all at the same time. I was happy for Tom because this is what we had been praying for, and I was hurting for my whole family because Loyce was gone.

I remember coming in the house to see my daddy sitting in a chair, just messed up and ugly from crying. I think he had tried to smoke a cigarette after quitting and was not feeling well. My mom was in the kitchen and, as I came in, I shared with joy and severe pain that Tom Rogers, one of our church members, was on his way to the hospital to get Loyce's heart. My mom was speechless. We chatted for a few, then I went to Methodist Hospital to visit Loyce a final time. I wanted to make sure the hospital was treating her body with care and concern… and they were!

As I walked in the room, it was very quiet. The noise from the life support machine was making that pump breathing sound as her existence was only because of this machine. I kissed her on the jaw where I could smell medicine coming from her breath and curl activator from her hair. I looked around to see a cooler on the floor. This is where her organs would go after being harvested. She looked like she was in a peaceful sleep. I told her that I loved her, and I would do my best to be a good Aunt to Casey and Tia. I then sat in a chair, watched her, and cried until I felt a peace that I can't explain.

I came home exhausted and got many phone calls from people that I hadn't heard from in a long time. I grew tired of explaining what happened. Pastor Rasheed called me and said, "Barbara, I need you to turn off your phone and lay down." So, I did just that. I woke up from a good nap and when I turned my phone on, I had a few messages from people that wanted me to call them back, but I couldn't. I was trying to figure out in my mind what was actually going on because I felt like I was in a bad dream and would wake up soon with Loyce being ok again.

My grandma visited from Lufkin as David had gone to pick her up in order to see Loyce a final time. I remember her reciting a list of items that were needed for the funeral home and while she was talking, my mom had a strange look on her face conveying that no one told grandma that Loyce was being cremated. I kindly said, "Grandma, Loyce won't need anything, she's being cremated."

"What do you mean, cremated?!" Grandma was shocked. "Yes ma'am, that is what she wanted and it's what we're going to do." Grandma was really sad, but I assured her that when she passes, we will do exactly what she wants." She reminded me that her white suit is hanging in the closet and she is taking all of her body parts to the ground with her. I expressed that we would make sure she got her wish. Then I thought

I would engage her in some humor. I said, "Grandma, have you ever thought about giving your organs after death to help someone?" She retorted, "Yes, I just thought about it. I want all of me in the ground!" and we laughed.

My mom chimed in and said, "Why would we be organ donors?" She observed that everybody starts out with the same parts and her question was, "Did you take care of the parts that you got?" If someone didn't take care of the body parts that they were born with, she said they would not take care of hers. I said, "Well Ma, that makes a lot of sense!"

*Loyce looking beautiful at my parent's
50 wedding celebration*

EIGHT

Sunday morning, the word was out that Loyce had suffered a brain hemorrhage and Tom Rogers was getting her heart. You could hear the air leave the room in a gasp with tears to follow. Most of my family was in attendance because we needed each other. We also needed the Body of Christ. Pastor Rasheed had my family come to the front of the church, and it seemed the entire church membership embraced us with a hug! The following Wednesday was difficult. I was trying to figure out how in the world would I make it without my sister, friend, chef on every Sunday, closet I could always go to, and of course, comedian! *What now?* My heart was in trouble, and I felt like I would die from heart failure. *God, who will we depend on for everything?*

Loyce had all of us spoiled. Brenda said she was on the list to pick up her kids from school in case of an emergency. She called mom every morning just to say, "Good morning!" She would buy my niece Monica's kids clothes and uniforms on a budget. Ronald could always go to her house, and she would make him comfortable, even if he was high, and even if she talked some noise in the process. She was there for us. She did laundry for Casey and Tia, and always cooked. Loyce also taught them how to cook. On a Monday morning, we had an appointment to meet at the funeral home to plan for her body to be picked up from the hospital and to find out how much the death insurance policy was worth.

David, Donna, Casey and I arrived at the funeral home. We came in happy as we could muster, because this was the moment when we were dry enough to make some simple decisions. I remember sitting around a table, laughing because they had some plans or packages that were ridiculous. The newspaper advertisement writing process was going strong until we found out that if all the names of our family members were included, it would cost over $300.00. We were cracking up laughing. Then we broke it down to fewer words, and it was still too high: $250.00. "No ma'am, are you kidding us?!" We were really laughing then, and there was a guy that said he had never seen any family act like us. Before we left the house, my mom said, "Don't go in that funeral home and let them talk you out of all ya money!" Mom said, "They try to get you while you're grieving." She was so right.

We finally did the minimum possible and made it out of there with an ad for around $80.00. David is my brother who has the know-how to get the program together, but we had to get pictures that would reflect her as a baby, in elementary, high school, etc. and a video was also made full of a lot of memories and more tears. I went home feeling sad and confused.

Loyce had a dog named Leah Aree Bryant, and she was family! Leah knew something was wrong. Loyce was a home-body and after a few days, Leah started crying and rebelling every time the front door opened. Leah would run to the door and just whimper, then I told Leah that Loyce was gone, and she was not coming back. I was in pain for her. Leah ate whatever Loyce cooked and was spoiled like the rest of us. Leah hated to be outside, but with so many people coming in and out, we let her out, and she was mad. So, she decided to dig a hole under the fence and start running away; but she would come back the next day.

One day, I was looking for Leah and found her in the front yard with a dog that I had never seen… Oh, Leah found a friend that she could have relations with! I went out that door and said, "Leah, if you don't get in this backyard, I'm going to whip you!" Leah looked at me as if to say, "I'll take the whipping." On another occasion, Leah was in the back yard and was still looking for Loyce. She wanted some attention. While we were looking at her, telling her not to go under the fence, she looked back and kept digging as if to say, "I'm going to have some more relations, and I'll see you in the morning." She went under that fence and messed her back up this time, but she didn't care. I said, "God help Leah, she is a mess with the rest of us."

Food started coming to the houses. Casey was employed with Olive Garden, and they made the best spaghetti, garlic bread, fettuccine, and salad. Casey said someone made it with love, because in her eyes, the food was not that good; she just worked there because she needed a job close to home. Pastor Rasheed came over to the house to assist us with whatever we needed. Brenda and Mark Haskins brought over catfish, fries, and hushpuppies. It was so good! They visited for a few minutes.

Loyce had a huge, funny personality

NINE

Saturday, August 21, 2010, was the home-going celebration day for Loyce Ann Lewis-Bryant at CrossRoads Covenant Church, 647 E. Pleasant Run Rd. DeSoto, Texas. We were preparing to have a memorial service for my baby sister. An usher was at the door to determine who was family and who wasn't. I remember Roderick Henderson saying that most of the people there were family, I said, "Yeah, it's a lot of us!"

I started greeting people that I knew from Franklin D. Roosevelt High School. The class of 1985 was in the process of planning a class reunion. CrossRoads seats about 500 people, and it was packed to the full; chairs had to be pulled out for additional seating. I was not shocked because Loyce knew a lot of people, and was loved by many. The church service began and specific people were on the program to speak. The ones that wanted to say something were able to write a note and leave it in a box. Keith Jennings spoke for the class of 1985. I remember him being funny, stating that the section in the church that was designated for the class was tight because of some weight gain, and then he talked about Loyce being very fun and humorous.

David was the spokesperson for our family. He talked about Loyce being a joy to have as a little sister and how she never judged him. He stressed the fact that she would be greatly missed and highlighted her gift of giving. He mentioned that one of the church members had been given the gift of life again because she was an organ donor. Then Darren Powell, her friend who drove from Chicago to be there, broke rank and was standing off to the side when he decided to be bold and speak. I don't remember a word of what he said because I glanced over to my daddy, who was needing to go out because he was overwhelmed. So, I motioned for my brother, Ronald, to take him out. As dad was getting up, Darius, my brother-in-law, assisted them as well. Then Shonda Pierce said there's no way she could just be there and not share how Loyce taught her to change a flat tire and the many mornings they enjoyed a cup of coffee. She highlighted the love their children shared and how much she cherished their friendship.

Janet Gadsden sang a song followed by Tia, Casey and a few more people standing to give God some praise. Then Pastor Burley Hudson sang, "I Won't Complain." As he sang this amazing song, we began to worship more. The song goes, "God has been good to me, all of my good days out weigh my bad days, and I won't complain." Then it was time for the meat of why we assembled. My nephew by commitment, Reverend Donald Ray Parish Jr., stepped up to the pulpit and talked about his Aunt Loyce. He talked about her buying uniforms for Devin from the thrift store, and the kids recently spending the night with her. She cooked fish for them when they should have been in bed. She even had toys for the kids in a corner of her home although her kids were almost grown.

I left church with my friends Kim Terrell-Fisher, Tammy Waters, Tammy Owens-White, and Yasmine Pearson-Williams. We went to Ojeda's for some Mexican food and talked about Loyce as we strolled down memory lane in our heads. Everyone had a good story to tell. I left them to go to the hospital to visit Tom Rogers. The drive was calm. I got to his room and was instructed to put on a gown and face mask to protect him from infection. His cousins were there, and we chatted about the miracle. I gave Tom a copy of the obituary. He looked so good and happy;

he said how sorry he was for my pain, but he was also happy that God had given him a second chance at life.

Then I went to sit under a tree for a few minutes with Paul. He is the one person that gave me the quiet that I needed. He really didn't talk about Loyce, because it was painful for him, but I just needed to be with him. He was playing Dominoes with his family, and I sat for a few minutes until I got too hot. It was August. I told him that the heat was too much, and I was exhausted, so we said our "See you laters" and I left. I went to Clio Clark's house, which is where I was staying because our house was full. I gave up my room for Ronald. The night was long. I went to bed, but kept on playing the last week over and over in my head, and in my heart, I asked God "Why? Why Loyce, God, she has children and she's the baby girl. I wish you had taken me if you needed someone." I said, "God, her girls need her. I don't have kids or a husband… not even a boyfriend. I don't understand." After a few hours, I heard God answer. He said, "Barbara, Loyce was ready." I said, "What do you mean she was ready?!" He said, "She gave me a 'Yes.'"

I started crying and went to the bathroom where I saw myself in the mirror. I looked a mess, like someone hit me in the eyes and got away with it. They were red and swollen. I said, You sho is ugly! (Color Purple) and I laughed at myself.

Sunday, the day after the Memorial Service, I was told by my Pastor to rest and spend time with my family. I did the opposite. I went to church. Pastor Rasheed talked about the memorial and also spoke about Tom Rogers receiving Loyce's heart, and I cried the entire time. I could not stand to Praise or Worship. I just cried because this was the second Sunday that my sister was not there, and it hurt like hell. Pastor Rasheed came to me during worship and said, "Barbara, I'm praying for you." and I said, "Thank You, because I could not pray." His response was that I didn't have to, and I continued to cry. Then I said to myself, *Girl, you should have stayed home!* I don't remember the service at all, but I was there.

Cathy and Tom Rogers at David's 50th birthday party, five months after the new heart

CONCLUSION

Eight years have passed since Loyce went home to be with the Lord. I have learned that God has been good to our family, in spite of her passing. He has shown the world that He still works miracles for those who believe. And for those who don't believe, I think He is showing them too, so one day you will tie your faith to Him and trust the journey.

After Tom's surgery, that went very well, he asked me, "How bad did Loyce want to get married?" I replied, "Real bad!" His response was, "On the very first day I got her heart, I had strong feelings of getting married!" Tom also said he was never a neat person, but he started cleaning everything with no explanation except this heart. My sister loved to work in her yard, so Tom started working in his yard. He said that since the transplant, he has become emotional about everything. I just laughed because Loyce cried most of the time about nothing! As the heart would have its way, Tom rekindled a flame with the love of his life, Cathy Hudson, and on January 1, 2011, the two became one flesh. This love was real and natural because they were friends for more than 40 years. Tom and Cathy were blessed to share three years of marriage until his body grew tired from complications with his kidneys (the heart was still good) and on July 29, 2014, Tom was released from time into eternity! To this day, Cathy and I are sisters. We fight in the spirit at CrossRoads Covenant and, this may sound crazy, but we are expecting another miracle. To God be all the glory, praise and honor that is due to His name!

See you in the next book!

 One of the last gifts Loyce gave me had a sunflower on it. At the hospital, the logo is a sunflower. The day I was headed to meet Melanie Davis with Triumph Press to finish this book, I walked past a fresh flower bouquet in a restroom… of sunflowers!

I continue to see them scattered throughout my life and it always reminds me of Loyce and the miracle at CrossRoads.

The sunflower is said to symbolize worship and faithfulness in various religions, because of its resemblance to the sun. It is associated with spiritual knowledge and the desire to seek light and truth.

Sign Up. Save Lives.

www.donatelifetexas.org

You have the power to donate life. By joining the Donate Life Texas Registry, you give hope to thousands of people awaiting the transplant they need to survive.

Registering to become an organ, eye and tissue donor records your decision to be a donor. Your generosity can save as many as eight lives through organ donation, bring sight to others with cornea donations and improve yet another 75 lives or more through tissue donation. It takes only moments, yet means a second chance of a lifetime. **Sign up today!**